CW00739863

# The C
## in Twenty-Five Days

by
Fr Francis Selman

*All booklets are published thanks to the*
*generous support of the members of the*
*Catholic Truth Society*

CATHOLIC TRUTH SOCIETY

PUBLISHERS TO THE HOLY SEE

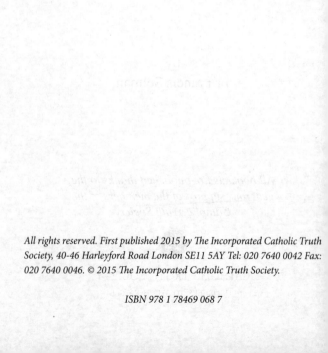

ISBN 978 1 78469 068 7

# Contents

# *Day 1: One God*

We first learn about God from creation. This is also the way we first learn about God in the Bible: "In the beginning God created the heavens and the earth" (*Gn* 1:1). When St Paul argued with the Athenian philosophers on the Areopagus, he said he could tell them who their "unknown god" was: "God, who made the world and everything in it" (*Ac* 17:23). The Church, quoting St Paul, holds that it is possible for anyone, just by the light of reason, to know that God exists: "Since the creation of the world his invisible nature, namely his eternal power and deity, has been clearly perceived in the things that he has made" (*Rm* 1:20). We can know God from his creation, just as we know that a work of art comes from an artist and reflects his mind: "From the greatness and beauty of created things comes a corresponding perception of the Creator" (*Ws* 13:5).

When we say that God created the world, we properly mean that he made it out of nothing. When we make things, we make them out of something that already exists, like a doll out of papier maché. But in making one thing out of another you cannot go on backwards for ever, always requiring something else before it. You must eventually come back to making something out of nothing. God made the world and the matter out of which it is made together. "By faith we understand that God made the world by his word" (*Heb* 11:2). "He spoke and it came into being" (*Ps* 33:9).

But why suppose that the world has a Creator? Could not matter have always just existed on its own? If there were just matter in the beginning, there would be no motion in the universe, because matter does not move by itself but only when something else acts on it. Nor can we suppose there was just a force in the beginning, because a force comes from something. If I put a spoon on the table, it rests there until it is moved by the table or the floor moving or, more probably, by someone picking it up by free will for a reason or purpose. Likewise, we can suppose that God freely created the world, out of love and for a purpose: to reflect his glory. In one thing being moved by another we eventually come back to a being that moves other things without being moved itself: an unmoved Mover. This will be an immaterial being, a Mind or Intelligence, who set in motion the world and continues to guide it by his providence. As an ancient philosopher, Xenophanes (c. 500 BC) saw, "One God…without toil he moves all things by the thought of his mind, moving not at all."

## ▶ Can science explain the universe?

The main alternative today to believing that the universe has a Creator is to say that its origin can be explained by natural science. The three most common explanations of this kind are:

1. the universe is due to chance;
2. it is explained by the laws of nature;
3. it is explained by evolution.

1. When the ancients considered the order of the heavenly bodies, they asked themselves whether this came about by chance or by wisdom, which presupposes a mind. We see that the parts and organs of living things have a function or end, but it is contrary to chance that things act for an end. Also, the end for which something exists first needs to be thought up, so comes from someone with understanding.

2. Likewise, the laws of nature seem to point to a 'law-giver', because laws need to be thought up. There is a *reason* for the laws of nature being as they are.

3. Although some people speak of the immense explanatory power of the theory of evolution, it is worth pointing out that it does not explain the rise of life in the first place.

These points allow us to see that natural science does not explain everything.

As God created the world, he has power over matter and so directs and governs the world by his providence. "Not one sparrow falls to the ground without his knowing about it" (*Mt* 10:29). He continually holds everything in existence as everything depends on the Creator for its existence in the first place; they only have the power which he has given them. If anything lay outside his sustaining power, it would fall back into nothingness.

We not only know about God from creation but also have received a more interior knowledge of God through what he has *revealed* about himself: the one God is also a Trinity of persons.

# Day 2: The Trinity

The doctrine of the Trinity can seem almost irrelevant to practical religion. Yet eternal life consists in just this, to contemplate the Trinity: "This is eternal life, that they know thee, the only true God, and Jesus Christ whom thou hast sent" (*Jn* 17:3). The Trinity is the fountain of all mysteries "It is the source of all the other mysteries of the faith, the light which illumines them" (*Catechism of the Catholic Church* 234).

At first the Church had no clearly expressed doctrine of the Trinity. It arose out of a gradual realisation that the New Testament, which took over the belief of the Old Testament in one God, also spoke of the Son and the Holy Spirit as God in the same way as the Father is. How can three persons each equally be God yet only be one God? The New Testament contains few explicit references to the Trinity, notably Matthew 28:20, 2 Corinthians 13:14 and Galatians 4:6 ("God has sent the Spirit of his Son into our hearts crying, 'Abba, Father!'"). Christian belief in the Trinity rests above all on the claim of Jesus Christ that God is his Father (*Jn* 8:54) and to send the Holy Spirit "who proceeds from the Father" (*Jn* 15:26).

In the fourth century, the Fathers of the Church, like Saints Athanasius, Basil the Great, and Gregory Nazianzen felt compelled to establish the doctrine of the Trinity when the divinity of the Son and of the Holy Spirit was denied. In answer to Arius, who held that the Son was less than the Father and the first-born of created things, the council of

Nicea, in 325, declared that the Son was "consubstantial" with, of the same being as, the Father and that he was not from nothing but "God from God, light from light". (If he were created, he would have been from nothing). The creed of Nicea was then extended at the council of Constantinople in 381, to say that the Holy Spirit is "to be adored and glorified with the Father and the Son" as God like them.

## ▶ Distinct, inseparable, one God

No one divine person is the other: they are quite distinct, but inseparable because each wholly shares the same divine nature, so that they are one God. They differ solely in their relation to one another. The Father comes from no one: he is the Unbegotten. The Son comes from the Father (*Jn* 8:42) and is the Only-begotten. The Holy Spirit comes from both as the love that proceeds from the Father and the Son in their love of one another. If the Holy Spirit only came from the Father, like the Son, the Son and Holy Spirit would not differ in their relation to one another and so be the same person. As all are equally God, who is infinite in his being, each divine person is as great as all three together.

In thinking of himself, the Father begets the Son, because he has a perfect concept of his nature, which is his Word, "the image of the invisible God" (*Col* 1:15) and "the stamp of his nature" (*Heb* 1:3). The Father does not beget his Son just once but is always begetting his Son, eternally. As "God is love" (*1 Jn* 4:18), God also loves himself. The Holy Spirit is the Love of God, who proceeds from the Father and the

Son in their love of one another. As St John of the Cross put it: "The breath of love which the Father breathes in the Son, and the Son in the Father, is the Holy Spirit".[1] Thus there is a communion of life and love in God, which we can share. This "love has been poured into our hearts through the Holy Spirit who has been given to us" (*Rm* 5:5).

When one considers the doctrine of the Trinity as a whole like this, one can forget that God was only gradually revealed as the Trinity. The *Catechism of the Catholic Church* says, "The whole history of salvation is nothing else than the way by which the one true God, Father, Son, and Holy Spirit, reveals himself" (*CCC* 234). The revelation of the Trinity was only complete with the sending of the Son into the world at his Incarnation, and the sending of the Holy Spirit at Pentecost. The end of God's plan of salvation is that we come to share the life of the Trinity (*CCC* 260).

Just as each divine person is in the other, so even now the Trinity dwells in us by grace when we know and love God. "If anyone loves me, he will keep my word, and my Father will love him, and we will come to him and make our home in him" (*Jn* 14:23). This is an effect of receiving Communion: "In that day you will know that I am in the Father, and you in me and I in you" (*Jn* 14:20). If the Father is in the Son and the Son in the Father, and the Holy Spirit in both, the whole Trinity dwells in us when the Son is in us. Thus "the whole Christian life is a communion with the divine persons" (*CCC* 259).

# Day 3: Creation

God is the "maker of heaven and earth, of all things visible and invisible". What are the invisible things that God has created? Angels and human souls, because they are immaterial.

God has created beings who are, like himself, purely immaterial: the angels. In-between angels and the material creation come human beings who stand, as it were, on the border of the material and immaterial as they consist of a unity of body and soul. If angels did not exist, there would be no higher intelligences between us and God. Interestingly, in an age which dismisses angels, people readily replace them with extraterrestrial beings in science fiction.

Angels are purely immaterial; they are "all ministering spirits, for the sake of those who are to obtain salvation" (*Heb* 1:14). There are nine orders of angels, three sets of three: Seraphim, Cherubim and Thrones; Dominations, Virtues and Powers; Principalities, Archangels and Angels (*Ep* 1:12 and *Col* 1:16). Seraphim represent the love of God, Cherubim his knowledge, and Thrones his judgements. The other orders execute God's plan of providence in the universe. 'Angels' are guardian angels.

All the angels were created good, but they all had to make a free choice of will for God in the first moment of their existence. The good angels always do the will of the Father in heaven. But one third of the angels rebelled with Lucifer, possibly the highest angel, and fell (*Is* 14:12). The

Devil or Satan "swept down a third of the stars of heaven, and cast them to the earth" (*Rv* 12:4). The fallen angels are demons and evil spirits, who constantly stir up discord as they have been allowed power over the earth for a time.

## ▸ The Human soul

God does not create human souls all at once but only one at a time as human beings are conceived. The human soul is created and infused into the body by God because it is immaterial; so, unlike the souls of other animals, it cannot be transmitted by physical generation. The philosopher, Aristotle (d. 322 BC) discerned this because when he considered where the mind comes from, he answered "it comes in from outside".[2] The mind is immaterial because it can think of abstract concepts like wit, justice, law and constancy without having images. As the mind is immaterial, it must be the power of something else than the body: of the soul that comes directly from God. "Then the Lord God formed man of dust and the earth; and breathed into his nostrils the breath of life; and man became a living being" (*Gn* 2:7).

We do not know at what point the soul is infused into the body, but the present sense of the faithful increasingly tends to think that it is at conception. When we ask at what point something becomes a human person, not having been one up to that point, we see that it is difficult to determine that point and, therefore, it can always be placed earlier. But even if it is after conception, we know that an embryo is going to become a person and should, therefore, be treated like one with the rights of a person.

The human soul is also immaterial because it transcends the body in that it can reflect on matter, as though from above. As the soul transcends the body in human beings, it is not limited or tied to it but can exist separately from it after death and thus be immortal. The arguments for the human soul's being immaterial are also arguments for its immortality. The questions of our origin and destiny, where we come from and where we are going to, are thus connected. The soul is immortal, because it is directly created by God. As St Thomas Aquinas saw, if the soul is not created out of nothing, it is dependent on matter; if it depends on matter, it cannot be immortal.[3]

It is because the human soul comes directly from God that we are made in his image (*Gn* 1:26) and that our proper end is to return to God. There is a contradictory tendency at the present time to exalt man by blotting out the Creator and at the same time to reduce us to the level of animals. Writers and scientists try to absorb us into the cosmos but we are called *out of* the cosmos to a life above nature with God. We are not merely products of evolution, and still less 'children of the stars', as though we have just come about through elements from outer space coming together by chance. Unlike the other animals, every human being has been made for a perpetual existence and, for this reason, each of us is assigned a guardian angel in God's providential care of us. "Do not despise one of these little ones; for I tell you that in heaven their angels always behold the face of my Father, who is in heaven" (*Mt* 18:10).

## Day 4: The Fall

Everywhere around us we find misery and suffering leading to death. How has this situation come about in a world that was created by God who is good? Some evils, such as earthquakes, are part of nature: these are physical evils. But the greater part of evils in the world are due to man's injustice: these are *moral* evils. The doctrine of the Fall shows us that the unhappy state of the world is not due to the Creator but is the fault of man. When Blessed John Henry Newman (d. 1890) looked into the world and found so little reflection of the Creator there, he concluded that if there was a God, and as there is a God, man must have been discarded from the face of his Maker and was "implicated in some aboriginal calamity".[4] We call this calamity 'original sin'. It is original because it occurred in the first parents of the whole human race. Our common experience of the absence of God is not because God does not exist but because of our fault. Newman himself was as convinced of the doctrine of original sin as he was of the existence of God.

The doctrine is simply stated by St Paul: "Sin came into the world through one man and death through sin, and so death spread to all men because all men sinned" (*Rm* 5:12). Death is the result of sin; all human beings die because the sin of the first man is passed on in everyone descended from him, with the exception of Christ and Our Lady. The sin that everyone inherits from Adam was an actual sin, which Adam committed. We do not know what this sin was except that he, and his wife Eve, ate of the fruit of the tree of the knowledge of good and evil, which they were commanded by God not to eat (*Gn* 3:1-6). Before this they were innocent. Original sin is not actual sin in their descendants but they inherit the guilt of Adam's sin as it affected his human nature, which is passed on by free will in human generation. Thus the whole human race fell in Adam, as he forfeited a gift of grace which had been given to him by God for all his posterity.

## ▶ Consequences of the Fall

It is not easy for us to see how we inherit original sin from Adam when sin is in the soul but the soul is created by God, who makes everything good. The solution seems to be that the soul becomes part of the human nature that is passed on from Adam, now in a fallen state. There would be little difficulty if the human soul were traduced, that is, passed on by physical generation, but we saw in chapter 3 that traducianism is not an option because the human soul is directly created by God as it is immaterial. If it is not immaterial, it is not immortal but perishes with the body. Yet it is plain that human beings are fallen: we do not fall by an actual first sin but we sin because the tendency to sin is already present, dormant in us. We do not fall by imitation of Adam's sin (this was the error of Pelagius, condemned at the council of Carthage in 418), but have it by generation. We only inherit the guilt of Adam's sin if original sin is in some way voluntary in us: it seems to be this because we voluntarily acquiesce in the sinful tendency with which we are born. Unless we keep the doctrine of original sin we cannot understand redemption by Christ, because we cannot say from what he came to redeem us.

The doctrine that everyone inherits original sin, with the exception of Christ and his mother, implies that the whole human race is descended from one original pair, Adam and Eve. This view is known as *monogenism*. The alternative is that human beings have derived from several original couples, a theory known as polygenism. The more obvious explanation why human beings inherit a similar set of chromosomes is that they all come from one original pair. Monogenism was upheld by Pope Pius XII in his encyclical *Human generis* in 1950, in which he said that polygenism was incompatible with revelation, namely, "all have sinned and fall short of the glory of God" (*Rm* 3:23). This would not be true if human beings were derived from different first parents unless these all fell, but even so they would not inherit the same sin. Also, unless we all come from Adam, many would be outside redemption by Christ because Christ would not share human nature with them from the same stock (*Heb* 2:14). The *Catechism of the Catholic Church* clearly supports monogenism when it speaks of the whole human race "as one body of one man" in Adam (*CCC* 404).

Adam's sin is called original sin because by it he lost the original justice in which God created human nature. Original justice means the original harmony and integrity of human nature, by which the 'sense appetites' obeyed the mind as the mind obeyed God. This integrity was lost by sin, so that the appetites no longer obey the mind because the mind is not wholly subject to God. As we know, the appetites war against the spirit and we do not do what the mind approves (*Rm* 7:15). Nonetheless, human nature has only been damaged by the Fall, not destroyed. As St Augustine described it, the contours of the image of God in us have been blurred, not erased.[5] The Protestants at the Reformation took a more pessimistic view of human nature, that our natural powers have been rendered almost incapable of doing good without faith. This is an error, since there is still some natural good remaining in fallen nature. The grace that was lost for us by Adam's sin is restored by baptism. Baptism takes away the guilt of original sin, which prevents us from entering heaven, but the Christian still has to struggle against the consequences of original sin, the disorder of our natural desires. By overcoming temptations, however, we become stronger in virtue.

## Day 5: The Incarnation

Who is Jesus Christ? Pope Benedict XVI has said that we learn who Jesus is above all from the way he prays in the Gospels. "I bless you, Father, Lord of heaven and earth" (*Mt* 11:25). At the Last Supper, he began his high priestly prayer, "Father, the hour has come; glorify thy Son" (*Jn* 17:1). In the garden of Gethsemane, he addressed God with the familiar "Abba, Father" (*Mk* 14:36). He calls God his

Father, because he is the Son of God. This was the answer of St Peter to Jesus's question "'Who do you say that I am?': 'You are the Christ, the Son of the living God'" (*Mt* 16:16).

Jesus shows us that he is God by his knowledge. He knew the Father as the Father knew him: "No one knows the Son except the Father and no one knows the Father except the Son and those to whom he chooses to reveal him" (*Mt* 11:27). Unlike the prophets, Jesus did not need anything to be revealed to him; rather he revealed in his own right. He was greater than the prophets (*Lk* 11:32). He also had clear vision of the things he taught, especially about the next life: "We speak of what we know and bear witness to what we have seen" (*Jn* 3:11). His knowledge was much greater and clearer than any man's: he is the Light of the World, who illumines our minds (*Jn* 8:12).

## ▶ Son of God

Although Jesus primarily refers to himself as the Son of man in the synoptic Gospels, even there, and not just in St John, we find barely-hidden hints that he is the Son of God. When he healed the paralytic man, in answer to the Pharisees' question "Who can forgive sins but God alone?", he replied "But that you may know the Son of man has authority on earth to forgive sins", implying that he was also God, and confirmed this with a miracle by telling the paralytic man to get up and walk (*Mk* 2:10). God sent his Son into the world, that he might save it through him (*Jn* 3:16). He had repeatedly sent the prophets, to recall Israel to himself, and finally sent his own Son, saying "They will respect my son", but when the tenants saw him they killed him (*Mt* 21:33-43). In this parable, Jesus openly refers to himself as the son.

Jesus was not just an exceptional man who was raised up to divine status (a view known as adoptionism, which is widespread today), but he is the Son of God who "descended from heaven" by taking human nature and becoming man. Thus the lowly Son of man is also the Son of God. If Jesus were just a man, it would not be true that "no one has ascended into heaven but he who descended from heaven, the Son of man who is in heaven" (*Jn* 3:13). He "is in heaven" at the same time as on earth because he is God as well as man.

How can the same person be God and man without any diminishment of his divine or human nature? Nestorius thought that Christ could not really be man unless he was also a human person; so he said that Christ is two persons. This error was condemned at the council of Ephesus in 431. He preserved the two natures at the expense of the unity of person in Christ. But if Christ were two persons, we would not be saved by God but only by the man who died on the cross. Thus the following council at Chalcedon, in 451, taught the unity of Christ's person while preserving the reality of his two natures by declaring "what was proper to each of the two natures was preserved as they came together in one person".[6] The solution of Chalcedon was to say that Christ has two natures united in one person, without any confusion or separation of his divine and human nature.

# One person

The unity of Christ's person needs to be preserved; otherwise we are not saved by God, because the one who died on the cross was also God. The completeness of each nature needs to be preserved intact, otherwise Christ may not really be God or man and atonement has not been made for sin unless Christ was man like us in all things except sin. When the Son of God became incarnate, a new person did not come into existence, because Christ's human nature never existed on its own; but an already existing person, the Son of God, *assumed* human nature into the unity of his person. God is only incarnate in one person, the second person of the Trinity. St Paul implies this, perhaps quoting a very early Christian hymn: "Though he [Jesus Christ] did not count equality with God a thing to be grasped, but emptied himself, taking the form of a servant, being born in the likeness of men" (*Ph* 2:6-7). Christ already was God, and he emptied himself not by putting off his divine nature but by assuming human nature.

## ▶ Human nature

He assumed a complete human nature, which the council of Chalcedon explicitly said consisted "of rational soul and body". We can tell that Christ had a human soul, because he experienced human emotions: In Gethsemane he was "sorrowful even unto death" (*Mt* 26:28). He also had a human will, and so two wills, divine and human, because he prayed, "Let this cup pass from me; nevertheless, not as

I will but as you will". Unless Christ had a human will he did not die freely and his death could not merit for us. It is only because he offered his life voluntarily that his death was the sacrifice which takes away our sins.

God became man in the womb of Mary at the moment she consented to the message of the angel Gabriel: "Let it be to me according to your word" (*Lk* 1:38). Christ derived his human nature from the same stock as the rest of mankind through Mary. He had one mother and one Father, not two fathers, because he had no human father but his human nature was conceived by the Holy Spirit (*Lk* 1:35). He was conceived in his human nature by the Holy Spirit, because he came to renew the human race by the Holy Spirit.

Jesus is one person, who performed divine things as man, such as calming the storm, multiplying the loaves, restoring sight to the blind. When he healed people by divine power, he often touched them with his hand as man. Thus he was truly God and truly man: he worked miracles and thirsted. As St Leo the Great (d. 461) said, "unless he is God the remedy could not be supplied, unless he was man he could not set the example" which it would be possible for us to imitate.[7] All Christ's human actions were saving as they healed many, but at the same time led to his death by the opposition they aroused. As the *Catechism* says, "Christ's whole life is a mystery of redemption" (*CCC* 517).

# Day 6: Redemption

Jesus is the Christ, the one anointed with the Holy Spirit, who was foretold by the prophets in the Old Testament. But the Christ first had to die to enter into his glory, because he is also the Suffering Servant. When Jesus said, "the Son of man came not to be served but to serve and give his life as a ransom for many" (*Mk* 10:45), he clearly alluded to the Suffering Servant who bore "the sin of many' (*Is* 53:12). The Suffering Servant was also likened to the Paschal lamb, because he was led to the slaughter like a lamb (*Is* 53:7). Jesus is "the lamb of God who takes away the sin of the world" (*Jn* 1:29).

God first redeemed his people from slavery in Egypt at the Exodus, when the angel passed over the Hebrews who had sacrificed a lamb and smeared the doors of their houses with its blood (*Ex* 12:21-23). Christ has redeemed us from slavery to sin, because he paid the ransom for all mankind by sacrificing his own life. As St Peter writes: "You were ransomed…with the precious blood of Christ, like that of a lamb without blemish or spot" (*1 Pt* 1:18-19). Christ himself died at the feast of the Passover. By dying for our sins, he re-opened the gates of heaven, which had been closed ever since our first parents were driven out of Paradise.

Christ interpreted his death as a *sacrifice* for us when, on the night before he died, he took the cup and said, "this is my blood of the covenant, which is poured out *for many* for the forgiveness of sins" (*Mt* 26:28), again echoing the words of Isaiah: "He poured out his soul to death" (*Is* 53:12). Christ's death was a sacrifice because, being sinless, he did not need to die like others and so could freely offer his life for others. "For this reason the Father loves me, because I lay down my life, that I may take it up again. No one takes it from me, but I lay it down of my own accord" (*Jn* 10:17-18). Although he was put to death by force, he freely died, because he could have called on legions of angels to rescue him from the cross. As Christ did not need to die, he alone could pay the penalty of sin, which is death, and so take away the sins of mankind. Christ's sacrifice is the perfect sacrifice, which replaces all other sacrifices, because he did not offer his possessions but his own body and life.

## ▶ Sacrifice and ransom

Thus his sacrifice atones for the sins of the world. The value of his sacrifice first comes from the life he offered, which was sinless and totally innocent; and secondly because this life was united to divine nature in his person. Henceforth no other sacrifice needs to be offered: it is sufficient by itself for the sin of all mankind of all time. Thus Christ is our great High Priest as man, because "he has no need, like those priests, to offer sacrifices daily, first for his own sins and then those of the people; he did this *once for all* when he offered himself" (*Heb* 7:27). When Catholics offer the sacrifice of the Mass daily, they do not offer many sacrifices but always one and the same sacrifice, which Christ offered once for all on the cross.

To redeem literally means to buy back. Up to modern times those captured in war used to be bought back from captivity and often slavery on payment of a ransom, and so regain their freedom. As Christ paid the ransom for us with the price of his blood when we were captives under the power of the Devil (*Heb* 2:14) and slaves to sin, so his death also *liberates* us. As the *Catechism* says: "By his Passion, Christ has delivered us from Satan and sin" (*CCC* 1708).

Because we became enemies of God through sin, Christ's death also *reconciles* us with God and thus makes peace: "While we were enemies we were reconciled to God by the death of his Son" (*Rm* 5:10). "Through Christ, God reconciled us to himself" (*2 Co* 5:18). He made peace, "reconciling us both [Jews and Gentiles] to God in one body through the cross" (*Ep* 2:16). Thus Christ's sacrifice on the cross fulfilled in one all the main kinds of sacrifice in the Old Testament: the whole burnt offering (holocaust), the sin offering and the peace offering.

But was it necessary for Christ to die for us, in order to take away our sins? Could not God have done this in some other way, perhaps by a mere word, without giving up his own Son for us? The answer is yes, but it was better for us that God chose this way. First, we see God's mercy in providing his Son as the sacrifice for sin. Second, it was right that someone who was one of us as man has paid the penalty and thus atoned for sin. Third, the Passion provides an example of every virtue we need in order to be saved: humility, patience in bearing wrongs, courage, and detachment from the world. Also we are more grateful, seeing how much Christ loved us by dying for sinners.

There is no resurrection from the dead unless Christ first died. He has conquered sin by his death, and death by his resurrection.

## Day 7: The Resurrection

The resurrection of Christ is the foundation of the Christian faith. "If Christ has not been raised from the dead, your faith is in vain", St Paul says (*1 Co* 15:14). If Christ has not risen, his death has not even freed us from our sins: "you are still in your sins" (*1 Co* 15:17). Only the resurrection makes his death effective for our redemption.

The natural way of reading the accounts of the resurrection seemed to the overwhelming number of Christians, until the nineteenth century, to take them literally as historically true. Since then many biblical scholars have questioned their historical truth and proposed that they were so written to express the belief of the apostles that Christ was still in some way present to them. This makes the inner experience of the apostles the foundation of the accounts of the resurrection rather than the resurrection the foundation of their faith. This cannot be, because the accounts tell us that they first disbelieved the women who told them that the tomb was empty. St John even believed *before* he had any 'experience' of Christ being alive again, when he saw the empty tomb: "He saw and he believed" (*Jn* 20:8). The Gospel accounts, then, are not an invention of the apostles' faith but rather its foundation. It is unlikely that they would have preached the resurrection at the risk of their lives (they were all martyred for this reason, except St John) if they had known what they preached was untrue. It is improbable that nearly everyone mistook how to read the literary genre of the resurrection accounts for eighteen hundred years after the event until some scholars discovered the right key for reading them. The evangelists did not write to mislead or deceive their readers but to instruct them.

## ▶ Mystery of faith

Christ's resurrection is at the same time an historical event, which physically occurred 'on the third day'; but it also transcends history as it was 'the passage to another kind of life' outside time. It is an historical event that can be testified by the sign of the empty tomb and the reality of the meetings of the apostles with the risen Christ, but it was not seen by anybody (the soldiers guarding the tomb slept through it) and no one could say how it happened (CCC 647). That is why it remains a mystery of faith.

Christ showed that he had risen in his body from the dead, so that the same body was raised up as was taken down from the cross and closed in the tomb, when the disciples recognised the risen Christ by the marks of his wounds. "See my hands and my feet" he said, and ate some fish before them (*Lk* 24:39-43). Although others had been raised to life again, it was to the same earthly life; but Christ is "the first-born of the dead" (*Col* 1:18), because he rose never to die again (*Rm* 6:9). When he rose, it was to a new kind of life as he was in a glorified state.

If Christ's body has not been raised up, the Church could not be called his body (*Col* 1:18) nor could we be members of his body, since we can only be members of a living, not a dead body. And the Eucharist would not now give us his *life-giving* body and blood unless his body had been raised up to life again. As we die in the body, death, "the last enemy" (*1 Co* 15:54), has not been overcome unless Christ rose in the body. "By his victory over death Christ has opened up the way to eternal life" (collect for Easter Sunday).

As he was in a glorified state, Christ was not seen all the time but only let himself be seen by his disciples for forty days after his resurrection. On the fortieth day, he appeared to the apostles for the last time in his body on earth and ascended in their sight into heaven. He told them to return to Jerusalem and wait for power from high (*Lk* 24:49) having told them he would not leave them as orphans but it was good that he left them, because he could not send the Holy Spirit until he had returned to his Father (*Jn* 16:7).

# Day 8: The Church

Many today desire to be a Christian but not to belong to a church. Why does one need to belong to the Church, in order to follow Christ?

No one can be a Christian without believing that God has spoken to us, especially through his Son. As there is one God, there can only be one divine revelation and, consequently, only one *revealed* religion. All other religions are natural religions in that they spring from a human founder. Divine revelation, however, is *objective*: it is not based only on inner religious experience but on *historical* persons and events: Abraham, Moses, King David, the Exodus and Exile, the birth of the Saviour in Bethlehem when Quirinius was governor of Syria.

The primary place where we find revelation is in Scripture. All Scripture is about Christ: God spoke one Word, and all the words of Scripture point to him (*CCC* 102). Christ is the centre of revelation, as the Old Testament points forward to him and the New Testament flows from him. As Christ fulfils Scripture, there is no more revelation to come after him; it was closed with the last of the apostles, who were witnesses of Christ's resurrection (*Ac* 1:21). Not all revelation was written down but some of it is contained in unwritten traditions, to which St Paul referred: "the traditions that I taught you by word of mouth or writing" (*2 Th* 2:15). Thus not everything that the Church teaches is explicitly contained in the Bible, but she does not teach anything that was not in some way known to the apostles. So called 'private' revelations made later, as to St Margaret Mary Alacoque about the Sacred Heart in 1675, do not add anything new to revelation but only highlight some point in it, often to inspire devotion.

Scripture cannot stand alone without the Church. First, someone was needed to decide which books are inspired by the Holy Spirit and so put together the Bible. This work was virtually completed under Pope Damasus in 382, although only formally declared at the council of Trent in 1546.

God has not only revealed himself but also given us the means of preserving revelation, so that its true meaning is not distorted or lost. But when disputes arise about its correct interpretation, who is to decide? When I see many Christian confessions, how do I know who can tell me the truth? I need someone with *authority* to tell me.

## ▶ Transmission of authority

When Christ ascended to heaven, he said that "all authority in heaven and on earth" had been given him (*Mt* 28:18). He received this authority directly from his Father, and he passed it on to the apostles when he commanded them to teach all nations and baptise them in the name of the Father, and of the Son, and of the Holy Spirit. Thus the Church has received a *divine* command to proclaim the Gospel to the whole world, and her mission continues the mission of Christ. The Church possesses divine authority to teach in the name of Christ, because she teaches with the same authority as the apostles received from Christ and handed on to their successors, the bishops, and so on all the way down to today. There is only one catholic and apostolic Church, spread throughout the world, because she is a communion. The communion of the Church exists where bishops are in communion with the successors of St Peter, whom Christ made the head of the apostles. Christ promised that his Church would not fail or fall as a whole into error (*Mt* 16:18). The Pope has the chief authority in teaching about matters of faith and morals that we need to know to be saved, because St Peter confirms his brethren, not the other way round (*Lk* 22:32). We continue to hear Christ teaching through the Church today, because he said, "Whoever listens to you [the apostles and their successors], listens to me" (*Lk* 10:15).

We do not just read Scripture for ourselves, which anyway was not possible for many before the invention of the printing press c. 1438, but require doctrine for its right interpretation. As St Francis de Sales said, God has not just given us a map and compass but a steersman to direct the boat according to the map.[8] Doctrine is essential to religion if we are not to be blown this way and that by every wind of new thought (*Ep* 4:14). Clear doctrines give firmness to faith. But they require someone with authority to teach them. There have always been doctrines in the Church from her first day at Pentecost: "God has made this Jesus whom you crucified both Lord and Christ" (*Ac* 2:36). The doctrines of the Church do not add to revelation but draw out and make explicit what is hidden in Scripture, often first when some point of faith is attacked, so that the Church is compelled to state exactly what she believes. Once we freely assent to the Church, we follow her because we believe in her divine authority. Christ promised to send "the Spirit of truth" (*Jn* 15:26), who leads us into all truth (*Jn* 16:13). The Church is "the pillar of truth" (*1 Tm* 3:16), because she alone stands up to the world in upholding the truth.

# Day 9: Sacraments

One may ask, Cannot I be a Christian without needing any sacraments? Is it not enough just to have faith and cannot I have a directly spiritual relationship with God by myself?

The answer is that just as God came down to us by becoming man, so we return to God through the humanity of Christ, who is the Way to the Father. St Paul tells us that Christ Jesus is the Mediator between God and man (*1 Tm* 2:5). Just as Christ healed people through bodily contact, touching them with his hand, so God now heals us inwardly through corporeal means, the visible, tangible signs of the sacraments. As power went out of Jesus when he was touched, for example, by the woman with the haemorrhage (*Lk* 8:46), so divine power enters us through the sacraments, by which we, as it were, touch Christ. Thus the sacraments are founded on the Incarnation of Christ; grace comes to us through his humanity, which was "full of grace and truth" (*Jn* 1:14). They are like the hand of Christ as they touch us outwardly and change us inwardly, as he continues his work of healing in us through the ages. As St Leo the Great said: "What was visible in our Redeemer has now passed into the sacraments."[9] What Christ worked through his miracles, Passion and resurrection is now effective in us through the sacraments.

The old simple definition of a sacrament as "an outward sign of inward grace" remains a useful one. The definition of the *Catechism* only expands it: the sacraments are "perceptible signs (words and actions) accessible to our human nature. By the action of Christ and power of the Holy Spirit they make efficaciously present the grace they signify" (CCC 1084). They have a sign (bread, water, oil etc.) but they are not just signs: they are *effective* signs, because the word of God also comes with power (1 *Th* 1:5). They *cause* the grace that they signify, for example, cleansing of sin by washing of water. They translate God's word into action. Christ acts in the sacraments: he baptises, forgives, offers the sacrifice of his body and blood in the Eucharist. And the Holy Spirit works in all the sacraments, just as Christ worked all his miracles by the power of the Holy Spirit. They always work together. Grace comes through the sacraments as Christ's humanity is united to his divine nature, the source of all grace.

The number of the sacraments was fixed as seven at the second council of Lyon in 1274. Although Protestants at the Reformation claimed that the New Testament only mentions two sacraments explicitly, baptism and the Eucharist, fairly clear evidence can be found for all seven in Scripture. The council of Trent, in 1547, affirmed that they were all instituted by Christ.[10]

## ▶ Why do we need the sacraments?

We need the sacraments for several reasons.

1. God comes to us in a way that is accessible to our human nature. As we consist of body and soul, we do not just have a purely spiritual path to God but God uses

external signs. Our spiritual life is related to our natural bodily life, so the sacraments match major stages in our life: birth, growth, maturity, choice of vocation, loss of health and death. As we are a unity of body and soul, we need to be part of Christ's body, the Church, in order to share his Spirit (cf. *1 Co* 6:17-19). Thus St Irenaeus (d. 200) said: "To sever yourself from the Church is to reject the Spirit."[11]

2. We are not saved by faith alone. We first need grace in order to have the virtues. Faith itself needs visible signs to strengthen it.

3. Through his Passion Christ has provided a remedy for all sin; but just as a medicine, once discovered, does not cure anyone unless it is taken individually, so we need to receive the sacraments to share in the saving effects of his Passion. Thus St Paul says, "they are justified by grace as a gift through the redemption which is in Christ Jesus, whom God put forward as an expiation to be received by faith" (*Rm* 3:24-25). We accept the Passion of Christ with faith by approaching the sacraments. All the sacraments derive their power from the cross since blood and water, symbolising baptism and the Eucharist, flowed from the pierced side of Christ on the cross (*Jn* 19:34). Christ has done enough, 'once for all', to save everyone but his work of redemption still needs to be completed in each of us.

4. No one can be sanctified except by Christ, because only Christ sends the Holy Spirit (*Jn* 15:36). So there are not different roads to salvation but everyone needs the sacraments as the normal means of salvation.

# Day 10: Baptism

We are saved in the same way as Christ saved us. As "the Christ had to suffer and so enter into his glory" (*Lk* 24:26), so we too have to die with Christ in order to come to his glory in heaven. But we only die with him in this life "in a likeness of his death" (*Rm* 6:5), sacramentally in baptism. In baptism we die to sin by being immersed and buried in water (now water is usually only poured over the head), so that we may rise with Christ to new life. This new life is grace, which had been lost for the whole human race by Adam. Thus by baptism we share in the divine life for the first time. By being immersed in water, and so dying with Christ, all previous sin is taken away, without any need for penance or confession. We have to die with Christ in order to receive his Spirit, because he could not send the Spirit until he had first died and been glorified (*Jn* 7:49). We all inherit the sin of Adam (except Christ and his mother) because we are all descended from Adam by nature, but we only become members of Christ by grace by being baptised into him. As we are baptised into him, we are also incorporated into his body, the Church.

Although Christ had no need of baptism because he was without sin, he underwent baptism by John the Baptist in order to show us the effects of baptism. Having gone down into the waters, which symbolise the burial of sin, when he rose from the waters the Holy Spirit descended on him like a dove, symbolising peace with God. Thus we receive the new life of the Spirit with the gift of the Spirit in baptism. Then a voice was heard from heaven, the voice of the Father, saying "This is my beloved Son, with whom I am well pleased" (*Mt* 3:17). Thus we receive the spirit of adoption making us children of God, so that "when we cry 'Abba, Father', the Spirit bears witness that we are children of God" (*Rm* 8:15). We are baptised in the name of the Trinity as the Father, the Son, and the Holy Spirit, all played a clear part in the baptism of Christ.

## ▶ The heavens opened...

When Christ was baptised the heavens were immediately opened. They had been closed since Adam and Eve were driven out of Paradise and were only opened again when Christ died (his baptism pointed towards his death). But we all have to make his death our own in order to enter heaven: "unless one is born again of water and the Holy Spirit, he cannot enter the kingdom of God" (*Jn* 3:5). Thus baptism is "the gateway of the life of the Spirit and the door which opens access to the other sacraments" (*CCC* 1213).

As we die with Christ in baptism, we are configured with his Passion and so receive a 'character' or special imprint, which can never be taken away even by sin but remains with us. This stamp sets us apart for the worship of God, especially for taking part in Christ's sacrifice offered in the Mass. It also gives us a share in the mission of the Church.

Baptism is known as 'the sacrament of faith'. It gives us the gift of faith and the other supernatural virtues and is accompanied by a profession of faith (the Creed), as in the early Church it often marked the conversion of adults from paganism to the Christian faith.

# Day 11: Confirmation

As baptism gives the Holy Spirit and his gifts, one might ask why there is a second sacrament of the Holy Spirit and what extra does it give? It is clear that from the earliest times there existed a rite of 'signing' with the Holy Spirit, which followed baptism. St Paul speaks of the 'seal' of the Holy Spirit (*2 Co* 1:22). Confirmation is firstly so called because it confirms and completes baptism. As the word 'confirm' literally means to make firm and so also strong, confirmation gives us strength to bear witness to the faith, especially before its enemies. Jesus told the apostles to wait to be 'clothed with power' before they went out to preach at Pentecost (*Lk* 24:49). Jesus said he was the one anointed with the Holy Spirit to preach the Gospel to the poor (*Lk* 4:18).

Confirmation increases the gifts of baptism and gives the 'sevenfold gift' of the Spirit in greater abundance as signified by the use of the oil of chrism. These gifts (wisdom, understanding, knowledge, counsel, fortitude, piety, and fear of the Lord) enable us to respond more easily to the promptings of the Holy Spirit in our lives. Wisdom helps us to *love* our faith, not just hold it. Understanding illumines our mind, so that faith does not just remain dark assent, but gives some insight into its mysteries. With the gift of knowledge we are able to relate our study of the created world to the Creator. Counsel guides us in making good decisions in life that will lead us to eternal salvation. Fortitude then gives us the courage to follow the path that counsel has chosen, and also to bear witness to our faith, especially when we encounter opposition and danger. The gift of piety is related to the old Roman virtue of *pietas*, which meant devotion to one's parents. Thus piety gives us devotion to our heavenly Father, so that we do what is pleasing to him, and confidence in prayer. Through the gift of fear we make ourselves subject to God and fear to offend him. Thus St John of the Cross says, "The perfect fear of a son proceeds from the perfect love of the Father".[12]

## Day 12: The Eucharist I

The Eucharist is the sacrament of charity, because we see in it how much God has loved us in giving up his only Son for us. When we celebrate Mass we do what Christ commanded us to do "in remembrance of me" at the Last Supper (*Lk* 22:19), when he loved his disciples "to the end" (*Jn* 13:1). Catholics have always taken Our Lord's words at the Last Supper, "This is my body" and "This is my blood" (*Mt* 26:26-28) at their face value, and so believed that the Eucharist is the true body and blood of Christ, really present though hidden beneath the visible appearances of bread and wine. We do not see Christ with our eyes but apprehend him truly present in the sacrament with faith, which is in things unseen. The senses do not tell us everything about a thing but only perceive the surface: faith goes deeper. Thus the Eucharist is called 'the mystery of faith'.

But how can bread and wine become the body and blood of Christ? No better or more simple answer can be given than words of the council of Trent: "by a wonderful conversion" (*mira conversione*).[13] When the Church began to speak of a change of substance in the Eucharist, saying that bread and wine are "substantially converted" into the true body and blood of Jesus Christ, she used the word 'substance' to oppose the heresy of Berengarius that the Eucharist was just a sign or figure of Christ's body and blood, not really his body and blood. This was at a council of Rome in 1079, over one hundred years before theologians began using the philosophy of Aristotle in theology in the early thirteenth century. It was only natural that a change of substance was later called 'transubstantiation'.

Bread and wine are changed at Mass by the power of the Holy Spirit, who is invoked just before the consecration, and of the words of Christ at the Last Supper, spoken by him through his priest, who acts in the person of Christ at Mass. As the words of consecration are the words of Christ, by whom all things were made at creation, they have the same creative power to change bread and wine into his body and blood. He who made all things out of nothing and so has power over the complete being of things, has the power to change the being, or substance, of a thing into something new.

## ▸ Transubstantiation

The words of consecration bring about what they say, so cause what they signify: "This is my body", "This is the cup of my blood". If bread and wine were not changed but still remained, Christ would have said "This bread is my body". But bread and wine are changed in their substance at the consecration, so that nothing remains of them except their outward appearances. Thus the signs of this sacrament are not bread and wine, which no longer exist after the consecration, but solely the *appearances* of bread and wine. It is wrong, therefore, to say that Christ is present 'in bread and wine', because this suggests that bread and wine are still present.

The belief that Christ is present beside bread and wine is known as 'consubstantiation'. But what is on the altar after the consecration and is received in communion cannot *really* be bread and the body of Christ, or wine and the blood of Christ. It can only really be one *or* the other: bread or the body of Christ; and wine or the blood of Christ. This is why the Church says that bread and wine are converted in their substance. Catholic doctrine accords with Christ's words, "My flesh is real [true] food, and my blood real drink" (*Jn* 6:55).

We believe the words of Christ, because they are the words of the Truth himself. As it says in the *Adoro te devote*, literally, "nothing is more true than the word of truth".[14] The same body is present in the sacrament as was born of the Virgin, suffered on the cross, was pierced, and is now glorified at the right hand of the Father, as it says in the well-known motet *Ave, verum corpus natum*. Once bread and wine have been changed they always remain the body and blood of Christ until they are consumed. Thus we reverence the tabernacle, because it contains the body of Christ. In this way Christ continues to fulfil the promise he made when he ascended to the Father, to be with us until the end of time (*Mt* 28:20). He withdrew his body from our sight but has left it hidden in the sacrament.

## Day 13: The Eucharist II

The Eucharist was 'the sacrifice of Christians' from the earliest times. It is a sacrifice because we re-enact at Mass what Christ did at the Last Supper in anticipation of his sacrifice on the cross next day by taking bread and saying it was his body 'given up for you', and the cup saying it was his blood 'poured out for many'. By this means the sacrifice of the cross is perpetuated until the end of time: "As often as we eat this bread and drink this cup, we proclaim his death until he comes" (*1 Co* 11:26).

The Mass is not just the commemoration of a past event but makes it present again; it re-presents it. The Mass is a representation of the Passion of Christ because of the separate consecration of bread and wine, as blood was separated from his body on the cross. The Passion is also represented by the breaking of the host before communion. The Mass can only make the sacrifice of the cross present again because what is offered in it, Christ's body and blood, is really present. Thus the Protestants who denied the Real Presence at the Reformation also rejected the Mass as a sacrifice. All that was left was a bare commemoration. The proper offering of Christ's body and blood at Mass does not come in the Offertory but *after* the consecration: "In memory of his death, resurrection and ascension, we offer you, Father, his body and blood, the acceptable sacrifice" (Eucharistic Prayer IV). The Mass is a *living* sacrifice, because Christ's body has been raised up to life again.

The Mass is the unique sacrifice of the cross, made present again, because one and the same sacrifice is offered. It does not add to Christ's 'once for all' sacrifice, as though he had not done enough to save us. We do not repeat his sacrifice, because Christ has risen, to die no more (*Rm* 6:9).

## ▶ Spiritual sacrifice

The Mass is not only the sacrifice of Christ but also of the Church, of the Head and the members of his body together. The priest alone offers the sacrifice as he represents Christ to the people, and the faithful unite themselves with him in the offering, uniting their lives with Christ's sacrifice in a union of heart and mind. The Mass is the same sacrifice as Christ offered on the cross but offered in a different, now unbloody way. Thus the Mass is a *spiritual* sacrifice of praise and thanksgiving for all that Christ has done to save us by his death, resurrection and ascension. We offer it daily, not because anything needs to be added to what he has done but because the work of redemption still needs to be completed in us. In the Eucharist, which contains the whole mystery of our redemption, we receive all the fruits of redemption: the forgiveness of sins and new life.

The primary effect of the Eucharist is individual union with Christ: "The principal fruit of receiving the Eucharist in Holy Communion is an intimate union with Christ" (*CCC* 1391). This union would not be so intimate unless Christ were really present in the Eucharist. We have no need to see Christ as he was seen when on earth, because he always remains with us in the Blessed Sacrament. As St Teresa of Avila says, he is "not visible but accessible".[15]

The Eucharist is also the sacrament of the unity of the Church, but this second effect is founded on the first. The unity of the Church does not arise from the faithful simply being united one to another but first from each one of them being united with Christ. This can be seen from St Paul's words, "we who are many are one body, for we all partake of one bread", which is itself a participation in the body of Christ (*1 Co* 10:17).

We cannot separate the communion from the sacrifice in the Eucharist, because what we receive in communion is Christ's body precisely as it was 'given up' for us, and we drink his blood as it was 'poured out' for us.

## Day 14: Penance

The reason why the first converts to Christianity at Pentecost were baptised was for "the forgiveness of sins" (*Ac* 2:38). The second sacrament of forgiveness, for sins committed after baptism, is that of penance (*paenitentia*, literally, repentance). The purpose of penance is to restore grace that is lost after baptism. But one may ask, Why do I need to confess my sins to another in the Church? Is it not enough just to say 'sorry' to God in one's heart without any need to go to confession?

To answer this question, we first need to understand a little about the nature of sin. First, it is an offence against God; but God reconciled us to himself *in Christ* (*2 Co* 5:18), so reconciliation with God is through reconciliation with Christ's body, the Church (cf. *Rm* 12:5, "we are one body in Christ"). We are also reconciled with God through being reconciled with the Church, because Christ entrusted the power of binding and loosing sin to St Peter and the apostles: the two are inseparable (*CCC* 1445). As the Church is a visible body, so we are reconciled with her by a visible sign. If we need to be restored to communion with her, we need to ask her through a representative. Just as when one part of the body hurts, so the whole body is affected, likewise when one member of the Church is unwell through sin, the whole Church suffers (cf. *1 Co* 12:26). As our sin affects the Church, so we are forgiven by being reconciled with the Church. It is not enough just to say 'sorry' privately to God, because to cease from sin is not the same as to be forgiven. The Sacrament of Penance corresponds with a human need to receive an *assurance* that one has been forgiven by God. This is spoken by the priest, who is the sacramental sign and instrument of God's mercy. The priest absolves from sin, but it is God who forgives. This power to absolve from sin is given to some men (priests) because Christ had this power as man, so could hand it on to men: "that you may know that the Son of man has authority on earth to forgive sins" (*Mk* 2:10). We also confess our sins, because, as St Jerome says, the doctor cannot heal unless the patient first shows his wound to him.[16]

## ▶ The Good Shepherd

The sacrament does not work unless the penitent is truly sorry about the sin: there is no forgiveness without contrition. Contrition is sorrow for sin that is inspired by charity, the love of God. Sorrow is not so much a matter of feeling as of resolve not to commit the sin again. It is right that we express our sorrow, so we give an outward sign of it in the sacrament of repentance.

The effects of the sacrament are that we are reconciled with God and the Church, and so have peace. We cannot speak peace to ourselves but need someone else to speak it to us. For this reason, Blessed John Henry Newman thought that if ever there was a heavenly idea after the Eucharist, it was confession. ('Lectures on the Present Position of Catholics in England', 1851)

In confession, we meet Christ as the Good Shepherd, who brings back the stray sheep. Like the lost son who was restored to full sonship on returning to the house of his Father, so one is restored to all former grace by forgiveness in confession. Although it is only strictly necessary for mortal sins, by which all grace is lost, it also helps to purify our conscience. Venial sins, our common daily failings, can be forgiven by prayer and acts of charity, which "covers a multitude of sins" (*1 Pt* 4:8).

# Day 15: The Anointing of the Sick

The Sacrament of the Anointing of the Sick continues Christ's own ministry of healing the sick. "He took our infirmities and bore our diseases" upon himself (*Mt* 8:17). We see from Christ's miracles that he came to heal the whole person, for in curing people's physical illnesses he also healed their souls by telling them that their sins were forgiven. Thus besides a sacrament for the forgiveness of sins, we also have a second sacrament of healing, the anointing of the sick. St Mark associates the apostles with Jesus's ministry of healing from the beginning as he tells us that on their first mission "they anointed many who were sick and cured them" (*Mk* 6:13). Thus we can take it that Christ himself instituted this sacrament.

The purpose of this sacrament is to strengthen the Christian in serious illness. We especially need to receive strength when we are weak through illness. When we suffer physically we grow in the likeness of Christ in his Passion. He himself was "made perfect by suffering" (*Heb* 2:10). This sacrament thus helps us to associate our sufferings with those of Christ (*CCC* 1521). It also helps people in the final stage of their life when they may especially be tempted against faith and hope in the face of death, thus giving them confidence in God's mercy. The sacrament also gives *patience* in bearing the sufferings of illness. As it unites the sick person with Christ's Passion so that he or she rises again with him, this sacrament also opens up the way to the resurrection. It is not, however, only for the dying but for the *recovery* of the sick person, if this be God's will. This is plain from the words for the anointing on the hands: "May the Lord who frees you from sin save you and raise you up."

## Day 16: Ordination

There are two sacraments of vocation or mission, which sanctify their recipients for the building up of the body of the Church and consecrate them for the duties of their respective states. These are ordination and marriage.

One might wonder how ordained priests are different today when it is common to speak of the general priesthood of all the faithful. It is clear, however, that although the whole of Israel was a "royal priesthood" (*Ex* 19:6), Aaron and his brothers of the tribe of Levi were specially set apart to serve at the altar (*Ex* 28:1). The levitical priesthood of the old covenant was superseded by the priesthood of a new order according to Melchisedek, because Christ being sinless could offer the perfect sacrifice for the sins of the people once and for all (*Heb* 7:15). Consequently, there is now only one priest, Christ, who is the one Mediator between God and men: "Christ is the source of the whole priesthood."[17] This ensures that it is always the same priest who offers one and the same sacrifice of the cross in the Mass. All other priests who are validly ordained by bishops in the apostolic succession share in the one priesthood of

Christ. Men can represent Christ as priest, because he is High Priest as he is man.

Although the earliest explicit evidence in the New Testament for an order of priests (presbyters) is found in the later, pastoral epistles to Timothy and Titus, the priesthood must go back to Christ, because the Eucharist was instituted at the Last Supper; so there must have been priests to offer the sacrifice from the beginning. The apostles were made priests with the command, "Do this in remembrance of me" (*Lk* 22:19). Thus priests were specially instituted to celebrate the Eucharist, and it remains true today that to offer Mass is "the principal act of his priestly mission".[18]

## ▶ Shepherds of the flock

There is a special sacrament of the *ordained* ministry, because some men are consecrated to God for the work of sanctifying the whole people, just as Christ consecrated himself to the Father at the Last Supper: "For their sake I consecrate myself, that they also may be consecrated in truth" (*Jn* 17:19). There is a sacrament of the priesthood because the task of preaching and leading the faithful is necessary for the building up of the Church; so some men are chosen to unite believers into one body. They first of all represent Christ, not the people, as they are not chosen by the community but by God: "no one takes this honour on himself" (*Heb* 5:4). Only ordained ministers are *shepherds* of the flock. They feed their flock by teaching and the sacraments. Priests are, as St Paul says, "dispensers of the mysteries of God" (*1 Co* 4:11), that is, stewards of the grace of the sacraments. When priests are celibate, this is a sign that they are dedicated to the work of Christ, the chief Shepherd who lays down his life for his sheep (*Jn* 10:11).

There is a threefold participation in the sacrament of orders. Bishops receive the fullness of the sacrament, because they take the place of Christ as teacher, shepherd, and priest, and govern the Church. Priests are co-workers of bishops. The special 'character' they receive at ordination configures them in a special way with Christ, so that they are made instruments of the eternal High Priest and can act in his person. Deacons are for the service of the word (preaching) and of charity. Ordained priests are 'at the service' of the general priesthood of the laity (*CCC* 1547).

## *Day 17: Marriage*

Marriage is not any human invention but was instituted by God at the very beginning of the human race. "God created man in his own image; male and female he created them" (*Gn* 1:27). "Therefore a man leaves his father and his mother and cleaves to his wife, and they become one flesh" (*Gn* 2:24). Marriage is part of the order of creation; it is not for us to decide what is its purpose or to alter its laws (*CCC* 1603). "So they are no longer two but one. What God has joined together, let no man put asunder" (*Mt* 19:6). Because the two, husband and wife, are one, the union is intended by God to be permanent until one dies. As Jesus said, Moses allowed divorce "but from the beginning it was not so" (*Mt* 19:8).

The natural union of man and woman in marriage was raised by Jesus to the status of a sacrament at the marriage feast of Cana, when the water of the old rites was changed into the wine of his grace. Marriage had already been seen in the Old Testament as a sign of God's faithfulness to his people of the covenant (*Ho* 2:20). As a Christian sacrament, marriage is a sign of the union of Christ and his bride, the Church. St Paul called it "a great mystery" when the two become one flesh, and referred this to Christ and the Church (*Ep* 5:32). Marriage is also a sacrament because it is the vocation of the great majority of people in the Church, which is built up by Christian families.

The ministers of this sacrament are the bridegroom and bride themselves in giving their *consent* to one another. The priest or deacon who conducts the ceremony represents the Church as a witness of the exchange of vows and gives the nuptial blessing. It is the consent of the spouses that makes the sacrament. Marriage is a sacrament because the married couple need special graces for their married life and to help them meet the difficulties of life together. The sacrament perfects the love of the spouses. Addressing married couples, St Paul says, "Put on love, which binds everything together in perfect harmony" (*Col* 3:14). Charity is the bond of perfection. The sacrament also enables the spouses to attain holiness, which is the vocation of everyone alike in the Church, through their married life. As St Paul said, husband and wife "sanctify one another" (*1 Co* 7:14). They are to love one another wholly, as Christ loved his bride, the Church, and gave himself up for her (*Ep* 5:25).

The act by which husband and wife love one another most intimately and become one flesh is also, in God's design, the act by which children are conceived. The Church teaches that these two aspects of the same act, the union of the spouses in love and the procreative power, cannot be separated. The act is always to be open to life. An act of love must be open to life, and the procreation of a child must take place as an act of love. This makes it clear that every child is conceived and born out of the love of his or her parents. Every child naturally wants to know that his or her mother and father continue to love one another. Thus it is best for children to be born in marriage and marriage to be a permanent union.

## Day 18: The Virtues

When a young man asked Jesus, "What must I do to have eternal life?" Jesus answered, "If you would enter life, keep the commandments" (*Mt* 19:6). The purpose of the divine law is to establish friendship with God: they set the boundaries for remaining in his friendship. There is no love of God without keeping his commandments: "This is the love of God, that we keep his commandments" (*1 Jn* 5:3). Jesus himself said that he came not to abolish but to fulfil the law (*Mt* 5:17). Far from limiting our freedom, Pope Benedict XVI calls them a "liberating power" in history, since we can only exercise liberty where there is order in society, an order defined by law.[19] Keeping the commandments presupposes the practice of the virtues.

We are human because we have reason, which distinguishes us from all other animals. We act virtuously when we act according to reason. Thus the virtues make us properly human. There are four cardinal virtues: prudence, justice, courage (or fortitude) and temperance. "She [wisdom] teaches self-control and prudence; justice and courage; nothing in life is more profitable than these" (*Ws* 8:7). Prudence is practical wisdom. It is the virtue for deliberating well about what to do and chooses the right means to the end. But one will only see the end rightly if one has the *moral* virtues (justice, fortitude and temperance). As a man is, so the end seems to him. It is the moral virtues which make a person good.

We need firm principles if we are to think rightly about moral questions. Prudence knows how to apply the right moral principle in each situation. Although the moral virtues dispose one for seeing the end of life rightly, prudence guides the moral virtues, since whoever errs about the principles will go wrong about the other virtues. Prudence also listens to the counsel of others. A prudent person, the *Catechism* says, is one who chooses in conformity with the judgement of his conscience (*CCC* 1780). Prudence takes care of our spiritual good and considers well the path of life and means that will lead to eternal happiness: "seek first his kingdom and his righteousness and all these things [our temporal needs] will be yours as well" (*Mt* 6:33).

## ▶ God gives his grace to the humble

Justice is rightness of will in not wanting too much for oneself or too little for others. It is the virtue which regards the common good of society. Part of justice is truthfulness, since society cannot function unless people can trust one another, and we cannot trust others unless they tell the truth. To worship God is also part of justice, since we owe gratitude to God for everything he has given us and done for us. As Benedict XVI again remarks, without the first three commandments about God, the others crumble as well: upholding the family, respect for life, and truthfulness.

Fortitude strengthens us, so that we do not give up the good of reason in the face of danger or persecution. We need courage to remain just and stand by moral principles. Fortitude gives our life constancy. It restrains fear.

Temperance restrains the appetite for sensual pleasure, especially the pleasure of touch in eating and drinking and in love, so that our appetite obeys reason. Reason and a clear estimation of reality are easily obscured by the passions, especially of love and anger.

The foundation and guardian of all the virtues is *humility*. Humility prevents us from thinking that we are more or better than we really are. To be humble is not to rely on one's own strength, and so is to put one's hope in God's power to work in us. "God gives his grace to the humble" (*1 Pt* 5:5). We need grace to practise and preserve all the virtues. Grace precedes our good actions, accompanies and completes them, for God "works in us both to will and to do" (*Ph* 2:13).

# Day 19: Faith, Hope, and Charity

In order to reach our proper end, which lies above nature, we need the supernatural virtues. These are faith, hope, and charity, which relate us to God. They are supernatural because, unlike the virtues we need for living with others, we cannot acquire them just by our own will and effort: they come solely as a gift of grace. They are also supernatural because they concern our relation to God.

Human beings are made to know the truth. The virtue of faith lies in firm *adherence* to the First Truth, God, as we do not have clear or perfect knowledge of God in this life but only see "dimly" (*1 Co* 13:12). Thus faith is less clear knowledge then natural science but it is about higher things and is more certain, as the light of faith, which illumines the mind, gives greater certitude than the light of human reason (*CCC* 157). Faith requires two things: first, a determination of what to believe. Thus faith is an *assent* of the mind to doctrines proposed by the Church on God's authority. Second, faith requires an inclination of the heart to accept what the Church proposes for belief. This second comes as a gift of grace from the Holy Spirit, moving the heart.

Faith is not just trust in God or Christ but is also in *doctrines.* The first thing that St Paul did after recovering his sight at baptism was to proclaim that Jesus "is the Son of God", a doctrine (*Ac* 9:20). We want to know who is Christ, where he came from, what he did and how he saves us. The answers to all these questions are doctrines about him. But faith *is* in persons who themselves believe and teach the faith, going back to the apostles and, originally Christ, "the faithful witness" (*Rv* 1:5), whom we can trust completely. Thus "faith comes from what is heard, and what is heard comes through the word of Christ" (*Rm* 10:17). Our knowledge rests on Christ, who is "the pioneer and perfecter of our faith" (*Heb* 12:2) because he saw and knew clearly what he spoke about. Faith is the foundation of hope (*Heb* 11:1).

## ▶ The anchor of the soul

The supernatural virtue of hope is a longing expectation of eternal beatitude. Hope is the virtue of travellers still on the way to their heavenly homeland, who have not yet reached their end. We have to hope right to the end. With hope we look to God for the help that we need to reach our end with him. Hope expects everything from the hand of God. We hope because we trust in the providence of God and that everything eventually works out well for those who love God (*Rm* 8:28). We are "saved by hope", St Paul says (*Rm* 8:24): that is, we put our hope in God and not in the false and deceptive doctrines of this world. Hope is "a sure and steadfast anchor of the soul", because Christ has entered the heavenly sanctuary before us (*Heb* 6:19).

Charity is not merely love of our neighbour, which might be only human love, but is first of all the love of God above all things (*CCC* 1822). The first commandment of love, Jesus answered, is "you shall love the Lord your God with all your heart" etc., and the second is "You shall love your neighbour as yourself" (*Mk* 12:28-31). But we express our love of God by loving others: "Whoever does not love his brother whom he has seen, cannot love God whom he has not seen" (*1 Jn* 4:20). Charity is the greatest of all the virtues because it unites us with God. There is nothing selfish about loving ourselves when we love our true good, which is to have virtue and grace. When we have charity, the Holy Spirit dwells in us.

## Day 20: The Beatitudes

Just as the ancient Greek philosopher Aristotle (d. 322 BC) began his *Ethics* by asking what is the end of human life, which he said is happiness, the reward of virtue, so Jesus began his summary of moral teaching in the Sermon on the Mount (*Mt* 5-7) by describing eight ways of reaching our end, beatitude, which consists in the vision of God. Jesus's point is that one can be blessed in this life even when not being well-off and comfortable as this world considers one to be happy. The Beatitudes, the *Catechism* says, give us a portrait of Christ: they "depict the face of Jesus Christ", (*CCC* 1717). We are more likely to transform the world and men's hearts by the Beatitudes than by the doctrines of Karl Marx or of any other ideology.

To be *poor in spirit* is to know our own insufficiency and so to be humble and ready to receive from God. It is the attitude of Mary, the lowly handmaid of God. It is contrary to the affluence of the Western world today and to avarice, which is never satisfied but always wants more. It is to be content with little. It sets our hearts in the right direction; not to look for treasure on earth but in heaven (*Mt* 6:20).

Blessed are those who *sorrow*; they shall be comforted. Many people, especially mothers, have sorrows in this life. This Beatitude gives us repentance, when we sorrow about our sins. It also enables us to share in the Passion of Christ, when we sorrow at the foot of the cross. But it also gives us the comfort of the Holy Spirit, who turns sorrow into joy (cf. *Ps* 126:5).

Blessed are the *meek* or gentle. Gentleness restrains anger and is needed for all the virtues, because it makes us composed, St Thomas Aquinas says.[20] It is not those who use violence but the gentle who will eventually possess the land.

## ▶ The justice and mercy of God

Who are those who *hunger and thirst for justice*? In the first place, not those who work for justice, who may be quite comfortable themselves, but those who *suffer* injustice, who are more likely to thirst for justice. This Beatitude is not so much about thirsting for justice in this world but for the justice of *God*. We can never have too much of this justice; we shall be filled with it in heaven. But all those who desire to possess uprightness in their own lives are blessed. Justice in society and in the world can only spring from the inner justice of individual people.

To be *merciful* is, literally, to have a heart for those in misery (*misericordia*) and so to enter into the misfortunes of others. This is what Our Lord did by entering into our human life. We are to be merciful as God is merciful (*Lk* 6:36). It is the condition of our prayer being heard: "Forgive, so that your Father may forgive you" (*Mk* 11:25). Mercy does not destroy human life but seeks to heal and restore it.

To be *pure in heart* is to see with a clear eye. "The eye is the lamp of the body. So, if your eye is sound, your whole body will be full of light" (*Mt* 6:22). Purity of heart helps us to see other people clearly and more simply, free from complications. It enables us to look at reality in a detached and peaceful way. "To the pure all things are pure" (*Ti* 1:15). It includes chastity of the body. It is also to serve God with an undivided heart. The vision of God is promised specially to the pure of heart (*Mt* 5:8).

Blessed are the *peace-makers*. Our first aim in any dispute should be to preserve peace. We make peace among others by first keeping our own inner peace. Christ made peace by the cross (*Ep* 2:14-16). St Paul told married couples, "Let the peace of Christ reign in your hearts" (*Col* 3:15).

Finally, blessed are those who are *persecuted for the sake of Christ*, as Christians are in many countries today. We need courage, the gift of the Holy Spirit, for this Beatitude. We may be disliked and shunned for bearing witness to our Catholic belief, but we are blessed.

# Day 21: Mary

Although one might find Catholic devotion to Mary excessive, Blessed John Henry Newman noted that where veneration of her has been neglected since the Reformation, belief in the divinity of her Son has also diminished. Thus the Catholic beliefs about Mary, far from taking honour away from her Son, strengthen belief in him. As Newman remarked, we praise the glories of Mary for the sake of her Son: the mysteries of Mary give greater glory to her Son. Catholic devotion to Mary fulfils her prophecy in the Magnificat, "All generations will call me blessed" (*Lk* 1:48). She is blessed because of the great things God did in her. We rightly honour her because she is "the highest honour of our race" (*Jdt* 15:9).

There are four main doctrines about Mary:

1. She is the Mother of God.

2. She was preserved from all sin by her Immaculate Conception.

3. She is ever Virgin.

4. She was assumed, body and soul, into the glory of heaven.

The second, third, and fourth, of these all derive from the first.

Mary was proclaimed the Mother of God (*Theotokos*, the God-bearer) at the council of Ephesus in 431, which condemned Nestorius, who said that she was only the mother of Christ the man. By calling Mary the Mother of God, the council made clear that her son is not only man but also God and thus preserved the unity of Christ's person. The first person to recognise that Mary is the Mother of God was Elizabeth who, when Mary visited her, greeted Mary: "What have I done to deserve a visit from the mother of my Lord?" (*Lk* 1:43).

## ▶ Without sin

The doctrine of Mary's Immaculate Conception, that she was without any stain of sin "from the first moment of her conception" (Blessed Pius IX, 1854), is implied by the angel Gabriel's greeting to Mary at the Annunciation: literally, "Hail, graced one" (*Lk* 1:28). Her immaculate conception means that she was full of grace from the beginning of her existence. She is God's perfect work of grace (cf. *Ep* 2:10). Just as, according to Scripture, the prophets Jeremiah and John the Baptist were sanctified in the womb, so Mary is all holy from the moment of her conception. Mary, however, needed the redemption of Christ as much as we do, because she was only preserved from sin in view of the foreseen merits of Christ's Passion. As St Francis de Sales observed, she uniquely enjoyed the state of innocence and the grace of redemption.[21] It was only fitting that God should prepare a sinless mother, from whom his Son took his sinless flesh.

Having conceived the human nature of the Son of God by the power of the Holy Spirit and given birth to God's Son, it is unthinkable that any man should ever have entered her. Thus Mary is ever Virgin, before birth, in birth, and after birth, as the Lateran Council in 649 under Pope Martin I declared. She remains indeed "an enclosed garden, a fountain sealed" (*Sg* 4:12). That Christ only has a human mother, not a human father, means that he has only one Father and that he is the Son of God.

## ▶ Mother of the Church

As Mary was free from all sin, so her body could see no corruption. Whether she first died and her body was taken up to heaven after a short interval or she was simply taken straight up to heaven, body and soul, was left open in the dogma as defined by Pius XII in 1950. One may believe either, but the stronger tradition is that she died, surrounded by the apostles, and her body was soon after taken up to heaven. An evidence of the Assumption of Our Lady is that no one claims to have her tomb on earth. The Assumption of Mary means that she already shares in the resurrection of her Son, as she shared in his suffering at the foot of the cross. Our resurrection from the dead at the end of time is already anticipated in her, who is thus a sign of hope for us. She is the woman "clothed with the sun, with the moon at her feet, and a crown of twelve stars on her head" (*Rv* 12:11). Thus she is the Queen of Heaven, raised higher than the angels in grace and glory.

We pray to her because, being sinless and thus more holy, her intercession for us is more powerful than that of any of the other saints. We can have special confidence in her prayer for us, as Jesus listened to her entreaty at the wedding at Cana (*Jn* 2:4-7). She is the Mother of the Church, as she was given by her Son on the cross to be our mother: "Then he said to the disciple [John], 'Behold, your mother'" (*Jn* 19:27).

No one on earth was closer to Christ than Mary. When we pray the Rosary, we reflect on the mysteries of Christ's life with Mary, "who pondered all these things in her heart" (*Lk* 2:19). Thus devotion to Mary can bring us closer to her Son.

## Day 22: Prayer

"Of all things needed for the Christian life, the most important is prayer."[22] It is like the precious ointment which Mary poured out on the feet of Jesus at Bethany. It is so easy to think that our time is better spent in doing other things, but the ointment filled the whole house with its scent (*Jn* 12:3). It is good to be reminded in an over active world that prayer is "the one thing necessary", and Jesus said that Mary had chosen "the better part" (*Lk* 10:42). Prayer is "a raising of the mind and heart to God".[23] It is healthy for us to raise our minds to God in prayer, because we are made for higher things than our merely temporal concerns of this world.

Why should we pray? Because it is God's will. Jesus said that we "ought always to pray and not lose heart", that is, not give up (*Lk* 18:1). Prayer is always pleasing to God, however poorly we might think we pray at times. We also need to pray, because we depend on God and are powerless by ourselves: "Without me you can do nothing" (*Jn* 15:6). We cannot keep grace without God's help. It is also charity to pray for others whom we love or who have asked us for our prayers or need our prayers.

## ▶ Continuous prayer

How much should we pray? Jesus says, always. St Paul wrote: "Pray constantly, giving thanks in all circumstances" (*1 Th* 5:17). But how can we always pray when we have many other things, work and duties, to do in our daily life? St Augustine (d. 430) answered that we can always pray by desire, and St Catherine of Siena (d. 1380) that a virtuous life is a continuous prayer. We should pray every day. Prayer in the morning sets our life in the right direction for the rest of the day.

There are two main kinds of prayer: vocal and silent. In vocal prayer we use words and pray with others. Silent prayer is our own personal, interior prayer. The primary vocal prayer is the liturgy of the Church, the Mass and the divine office, which is the prayer of the Church and so the prayer of Christ, who prayed the psalms himself. When we pray the psalms with the Church, we pray with and in Christ, because so many of the psalms are about the Christ and his sufferings. Vocal and silent prayer complement one another: the liturgy of the Church nourishes our personal prayer and silent prayer helps us to pray the liturgy more interiorly.

## ▶ Prayer brings peace

We do not need to pray with words all the time; friends can be silent with one another. Jesus tells us to enter the chamber of our heart and to shut the door to the world outside when we pray (*Mt* 6:6). We can begin silent prayer by putting ourselves in the presence of God: "We believe that God is present everywhere", St Benedict (d. 548) wrote.[24] Prayer is just trying to remain in that presence. Prayer is not just speaking to God but also listening to God and giving him space to speak to us. It is not so much what we do but God's work in us. "Be still and know that I am God" (*Ps* 45:10). All we need to bring to prayer is patience in waiting and confidence.

In prayer we exercise the three supernatural virtues. Prayer is founded on faith that all things are in the hand of God. Prayer expresses our hope because we hope to receive from God what we pray for. Hope prevents us from being discouraged in prayer. The end of prayer is to grow in charity. "What we seek most of all in prayer is to be united to God", St Thomas Aquinas says.[25] Charity unites us with God.

We have many things to pray for, our own needs and the needs of others, but Jesus reminds us that what we are to pray for most of all is the gift of the Holy Spirit: "How much more will the heavenly Father give the Holy Spirit to those who ask him" (*Lk* 11:13). The Holy Spirit is "the interior Master of Christian prayer" (*CCC* 2672).

Prayer is never wasted. We can do so much good for the world by prayer, because prayer brings it peace.

## Day 23: Eternal Life

The end of human life is happiness: God has created us to share his blessed life (*CCC* 1). God has put in everyone a desire for happiness, which can only be fulfilled by God.

When we die, our soul is separated from the body and enters eternal life. At the moment of death we know our judgement by God: Men "die once, and after that comes judgement" (*Heb* 9:27). There are two judgements: a private one known only to the individual at the moment of death; and a general one, the Last Judgement, on the Last Day at the end of the world, when the Son of man will come again in glory with his angels, to judge the living and the dead, and all will be made known (cf. *Mt* 25:1).

At death we shall know whether we have deserved to enter heaven or whether we are damned to eternal suffering in hell. Those who are already saints receive the vision of God and enter the joy of their Master straightaway. The damned also depart to hell straightaway, as they cannot anymore change their mind or repent and so are for ever irredeemable. The time for accepting grace comes to an end at death (*CCC* 1022). As the *Catechism* says, God does not so much judge people as they judge themselves by refusing the offer of grace in this life (*CCC* 679). But many who deserve heaven are not yet ready to enter it or to see God face-to-face immediately and so have to wait in a place of purification, which we call purgatory.

Christians have from earliest times prayed for the dead. This was not for those who had already reached heaven and no longer need our prayer; nor for those in hell, who cannot be helped by our prayers as they cannot anymore be redeemed. So it was for souls in another place: in purgatory. We need to be purified to see God: "Blessed are the pure of heart, for they shall see God" (*Mt* 5:8). We can be purified by suffering and penance even in this life. Purgatory is the place where we pay the debt of penance for our sins that we have left undone in this life. Thus the suffering in purgatory is not only purifying but also expiates our sins. Those in purgatory can be helped to pay their debt by the prayers of the living, especially by the sacrifice of the Mass, as Christ took away our sins by his death on the cross. Although they suffer, the souls in purgatory have the sure hope of coming to heaven. There is only one way out of purgatory: into heaven. Thus the suffering of purgatory is quite different from suffering eternally in hell.

## ▸ Is anyone in hell?

Is any createure in hell? Certainly, the Devil and the fallen angels. We do not know who else is in it, but Christ's words about weeping and grinding of teeth (*Mt* 22:13) and being cast into the outer darkness (*Mt* 25:30) are too frequent for us not to take them seriously. The way to life is narrow, and few find it (*Mt* 7:14). As the reward of virtue is eternal happiness, so the desert of vice is misery, unless it is repented. As the blessed would not think of turning away from their joy, so the will of those in hell is also fixed, turned away from God. To be separated from God is misery, because it is to miss our end and destiny. Jesus speaks of unending remorse (*Mk* 9:48). He also said that there is a great gulf fixed between those in heaven and those suffering eternal thirst (for God), which no one can cross (*Lk* 16:26).

There is little in the Gospel to support universalism, the view that, at the end, everyone will be saved and no one remain in hell. God respects our freedom and does not bend back our wills to him against our will. If it seems unjust that anyone should suffer in eternity for what they did in this brief life, St Gregory the Great (d. 604) said that it was unlikely that unremitting sinners would change if they were given another life.[26] St Justin (martyr, d. 155) thought that if vice is not punished in eternal life, either God has no care of men or he condones evil.[27] If he has no care of what we do, there is no divine providence for us.

We help those in purgatory with our prayers and are, in turn, helped by the prayers of the saints in heaven. St Thérèse of Lisieux (d. 1897) said: "My heaven will be to do good on earth."

## Day 24: The Resurrection of the Dead

If God can make the world, he can remake it: he can raise up the dead, as Jesus in his life on earth raised up the son of the widow of Nain (*Lk* 7:14) and Lazarus (*Jn* 11:44). There is no proper hope of my remaining for ever as someone with the same human nature, consisting of body and soul, if only my soul is immortal but my body is not raised up. As St Thomas Aquinas said, "If only my soul is saved, I am not saved", for I am not just my soul.[28] Thus the resurrection of the body means that the whole person is redeemed and saved. The early Christian apologist, Athenagoras (c. 180), thought it reasonable to expect the resurrection of the dead if the soul is immortal, otherwise I do not remain as a human being unless my body is also raised up.[29] As we do our deeds in the body in this life, so the body will share in reward or punishment in eternity.

There are two resurrections: a spiritual one in this life and a bodily one at the end of time. Jesus speaks of those who hear his word and cross over from death to life (*Jn* 5:24). This is a spiritual resurrection by faith in this life. Then he speaks of everyone coming forth from the tombs, some to the resurrection of life, some to the resurrection of judgement (*Jn* 5:29). This is the resurrection of the body when Jesus comes again. Everyone will rise again, the just and the unjust (*Ac* 24:15), or some to everlasting glory and some to everlasting disgrace (*Dn* 12:2). St Paul said that the error of Hymenaeus and Philetas, that there is only a spiritual resurrection now, not a future resurrection, was like a "gangrene" (*2 Tm* 2:17).

## ▶ Resurrection of the body

Some people today, because they do not believe we have an immortal soul, think that our resurrection happens straightaway when we die. This is contrary to the Church's teaching that everyone, except Mary, has to wait until the general judgement for the resurrection of their body. The saints already enjoy the vision of God in heaven but still await the resurrection.[30] Catholic faith is just what Martha said about her brother, Lazarus: "I know that he will rise again on the last day" (*Jn* 11:24).

What kind of bodies will we get back at the resurrection? St Paul says it will be as different as a grain of wheat that is sown in the ground and the full grown blade (*1 Co* 15:36-37). As star differs from star in glory, so the earthly and heavenly body (*1 Co* 15:41). When St Paul says that we will have "spiritual" bodies (*1 Co* 15:44), he does not mean that we will be just spirits but that the glorious body will be wholly subject to the spirit. Only the blessed will have glorious bodies. The glory of the soul, depending on one's degree of grace and charity, will overflow into the body. But it will be a body of the same nature, otherwise it is not me who is raised up, but in a different state.

Belief in reincarnation is incompatible with the Christian belief about the resurrection. Our resurrection will be just like Christ's, who rose to die no more (*Rm* 6:9). We only die once and do not return to this life. Our lowly body will be transformed to be like his glorious body by the power of him who has power over everything (*Ph* 3:21).

# Day 25: Catholicism and Other Religions

Many people today think that one religion is as true as another and it does not much matter which one chooses. From early on Christians recognised that the divine Word had sown 'seeds of truth' among the pagans, and the Church today agrees that elements of truth are found in other religions. But there is no truth in another religion which is not also contained in the revelation of the Bible; otherwise it would not be true that the fullness of God's revelation came in his Son, Jesus Christ. Although one commonly hears it said that followers of different religions all worship the same God, some (Hindus) believe in several gods, and others (Buddhists) do not believe in a personal god. In no other religion, apart from the Christian, is Christ the Way. The differences of religions are greater than is often appreciated.

## ▶ Catholics believe…

There is more to religion than just being an ethical way or a way of peace. True religion is not just the expression of an inner longing of the human spirit for God: it is based on a *creed*. The following points may be highlighted:

1. The one God has revealed himself as the Trinity through the sending of the Son and the Holy Spirit.

2. We *need to be saved* from sin. Only Jesus Christ can save us, because he alone has offered the one sacrifice that takes away the sin of the world. For this reason, "there is no other name by which men can be saved" (*Ac* 4:12).

3. We can have a life of *union with Christ* through sharing in the Eucharist.

4. Through the sacraments we are filled with grace from above; we do not just gain salvation through our natural powers.

No other founder of a religion than Jesus Christ could say that he came from above (*Jn* 8:23) and knew where he was going to. Only someone who has come back from the dead can show us the way to everlasting life.

# Endnotes

[1] *Spiritual Canticle* 39,3.

[2] *De Generatione Animalium* II c.3.

[3] *Summa Theologiae (ST)* Ia 118,2.

[4] *Apologia pro Vita sua*, c.5.

[5] *De spiritu et littera* 24,48.

[6] Neuner-Dupuis, *The Christian Faith*, 615.

[7] *Sermon on the Nativity* 1,3.

[8] *The Controversies* Pt II art. 3 c.1.

[9] *Sermon* 74,2.

[10] Neuner-Dupuis, 1311.

[11] *Adversus haereses* 3 c.24, 1.

[12] *Spiritual Canticle* 17, 2.

[13] Neuner-Dupuis, 1527.

[14] *Didache*, 11

[15] *The Way of Perfection*, c. 34, 8.

[16] *In Ecclesiastes* 10,11.

[17] Thomas Aquinas, *ST* 3a 22,4.

[18] Vatican II, *Presbyterorum ordinis*, 14.

[19] *Truth and Tolerance*, 255.

[20] *ST* 2a 2ae 157, 4.

[21] *Treatise of the Love of God*, II c. 6.

[22] Thomas Aquinas, *Expositio super 1 ad Timotheum*, c. 2 lect. 1.

[23] St John Damascene, *De Fide Orthodoxa*, III c. 24.

[24] *Rule*, c. 19.

[25] *ST* 2a 2ae 83, 1 ad 2.

[26] *Moralia in Job*, 34, 36.

[27] *Apologia*, II 9.

[28] *Expositio super 1 ad Corinthos*, c. 15 lect. 2.

[29] *The Resurrection of the Dead*, 15.

[30] Cf. Benedict XII, *Benedictus Deus* (1326).